DEATH BY THE BLACK DEATH

Ancient History 5th Grade

Children's History

BABY PROFESSOR

EDUCATION KIDS

Speedy Publishing LLC

40 E. Main St. #1156

Newark, DE 19711

www.speedypublishing.com

Copyright 2017

The Black Death was the name of a horrible disease which spread through Europe between 1347 and 1359. It was very contagious and there was no cure. Read further to learn how it started, how horrible it was, what the symptoms were, and how to prevent it.

HOW DID IT START?

This illness started once 12 Genoese ships docked in Messina at the Sicilian port after a lengthy journey through the Black Sea. As people gathered at the docks to greet these ships, they found a horrifying surprise; almost all of the sailors were dead, and the sailors that were still alive were deathly ill.

They had a high fever, could not keep food down, and they were delirious with pain. But the strangest thing was that they were all covered with unknown black boils, oozing pus and blood, and that is why it became known as the "Black Death". The local authorities immediately demanded that these "death ships" be removed from the harbor, but the order came too late.

WHAT WAS THE BLACK DEATH?

Scientists today know that this illness, known now as the plague, spreads by a bacillus named Yersina pestis, named for Alexandre Yersin, the French biologist who discovered the germ towards the end of the 19th century.

Alexandre Yersin

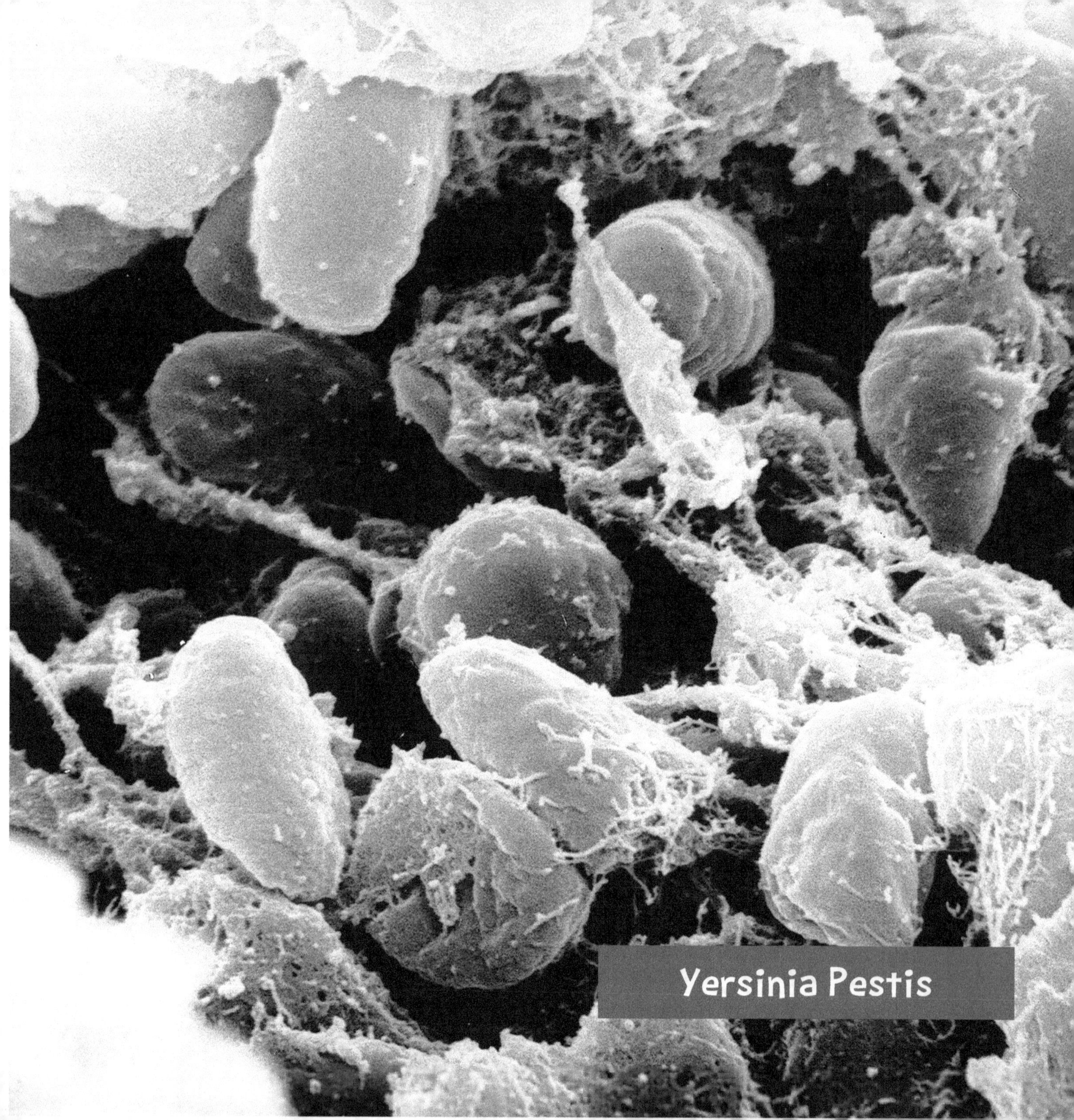
Yersinia Pestis

They understand that it travels pneumonically from person to person (through the air), and also can travel by bites from infected rats and fleas. Both pests were found everywhere in Europe during this era, but more predominately found on ships - which is how the plague made it from one port to another.

Not too long after striking Messina, it spread to the Marseilles port in France and the Tunis port of North Africa. It then reached Florence and Rome, two cities that were at the center of elaborate trade routes. At the middle of 1348, it had stricken London, Lyon, Bordeaux, and Paris.

Yersinia Pestis Bacteria

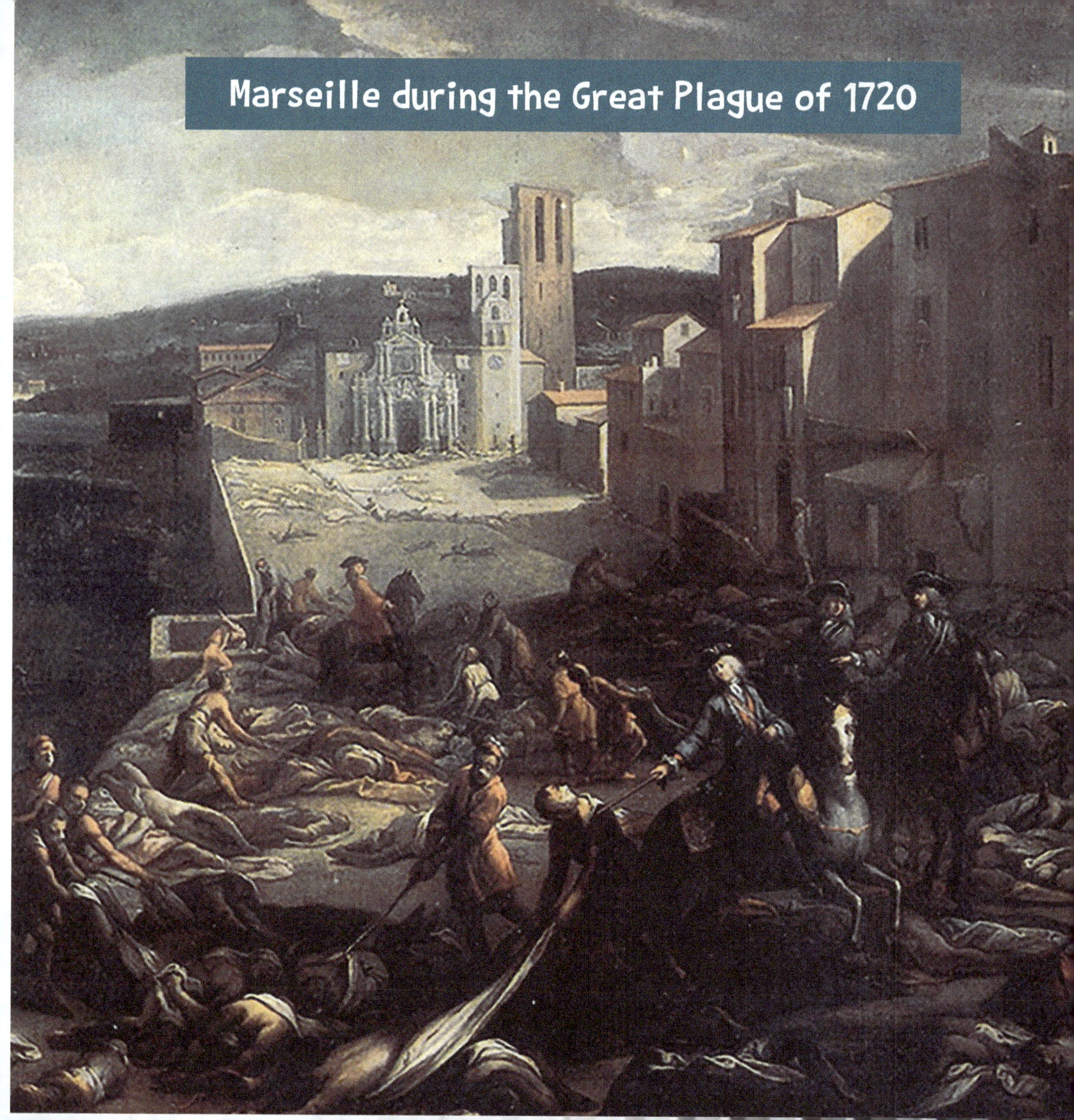

Marseille during the Great Plague of 1720

The plague was not named Black Death for many years. Some people believe that it was given this name because of the discoloration that it caused to the skin during the later stages of its progress. However, more than likely it was named "Black" because it reflected the horrible and dark period in history.

SYMPTOMS

The most significant symptom is an enlarged, infected, and painful lymph node, otherwise known as buboes. Once transmitted with the bite of a flea that has been infected with the Y. pestis bacteria, it becomes localized in the affected lymph node and begins to colonize and reproduce. These buboes are typically found in the neck area, the groin area, the upper femoral area, and in the armpits. Another symptom can be Acral gangrene of the nose, lips, toes, and fingers.

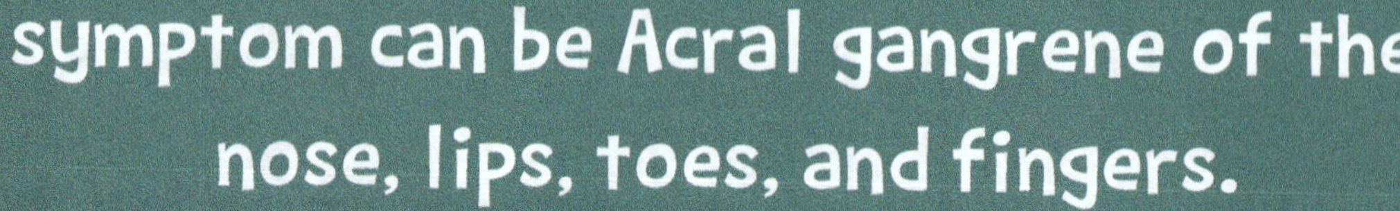

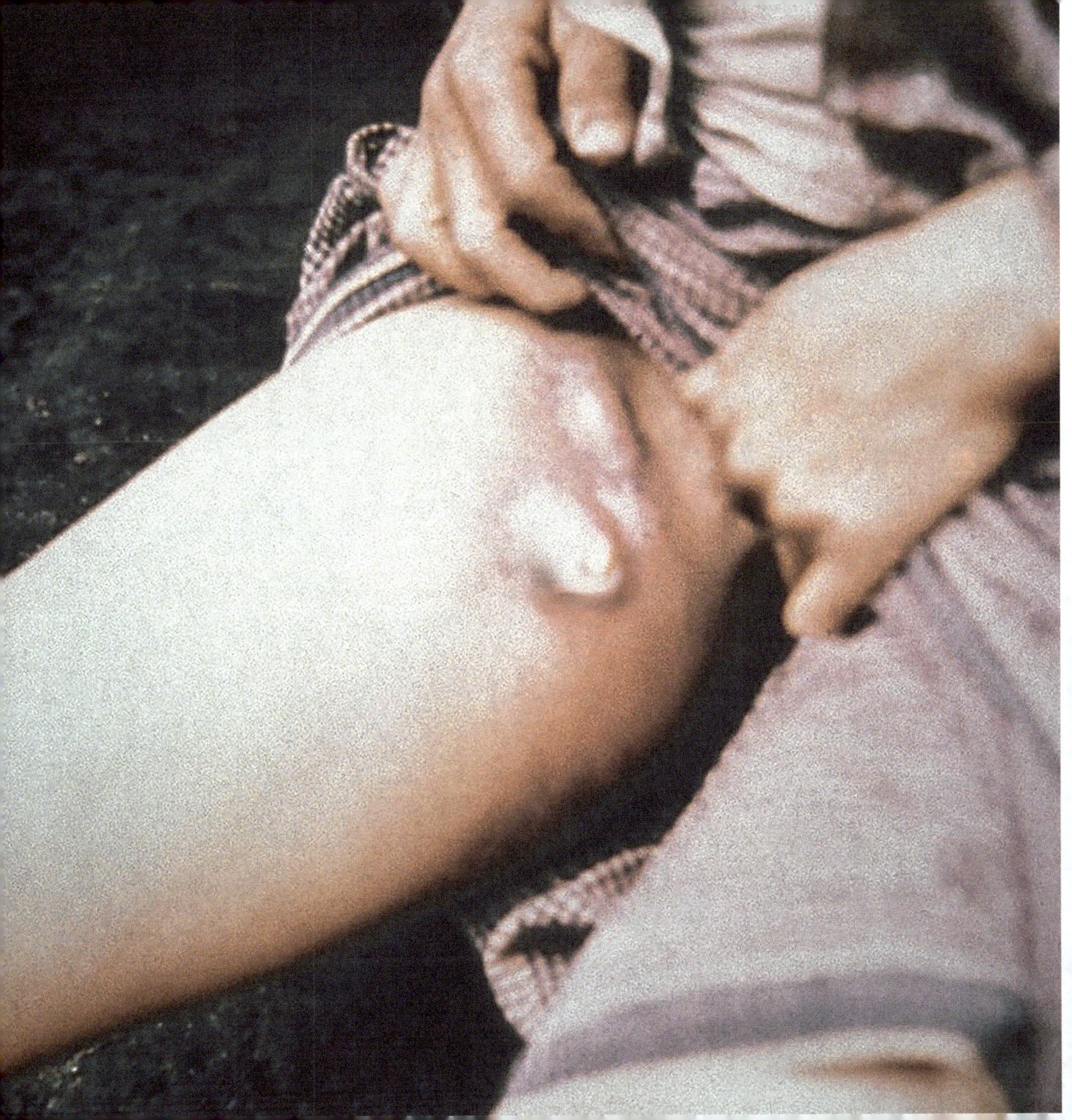

Due to the bite-sized transmission mode, the plague is frequently found to be the first of a series of illnesses and the symptoms suddenly appear within a few days after the exposure.

Symptoms may include: chills, a general ill feeling (malaise), a high fever of 39 degrees Celsius or 102 degrees Fahrenheit, cramping of the muscles, seizures, buboes (swelling of the lymph nodes often found near the site of the original infection, pain in the area prior to the swelling, Gangrene of the extremities such as fingers, toes, lips and the tip of the nose.

Quarantine area, bubonic plague

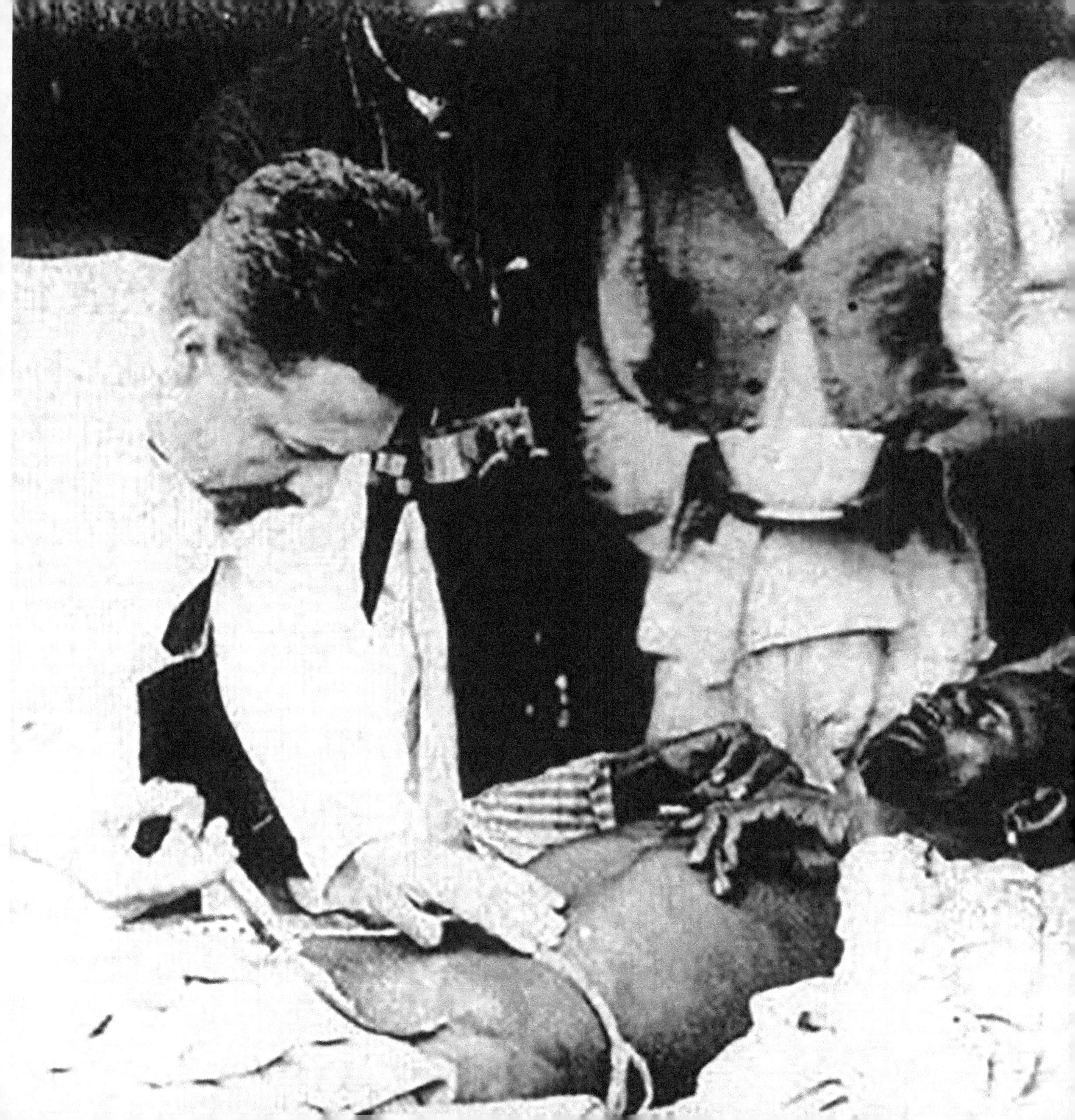

Additional symptoms might be coughing, achiness of the limbs, vomiting blood continuously, heavy breathing, and decomposition or decay of skin causing extreme pain while a person remains alive. Other symptoms include, delirium, black dots throughout the body (lenticulae), gastrointestinal issues, extreme fatigue, and coma.

Keep in mind that just because you might ex-
perience one or more of these symptoms, it
does not indicate that you have the plague,
but be sure to let your parents know that you
are not feeling well.

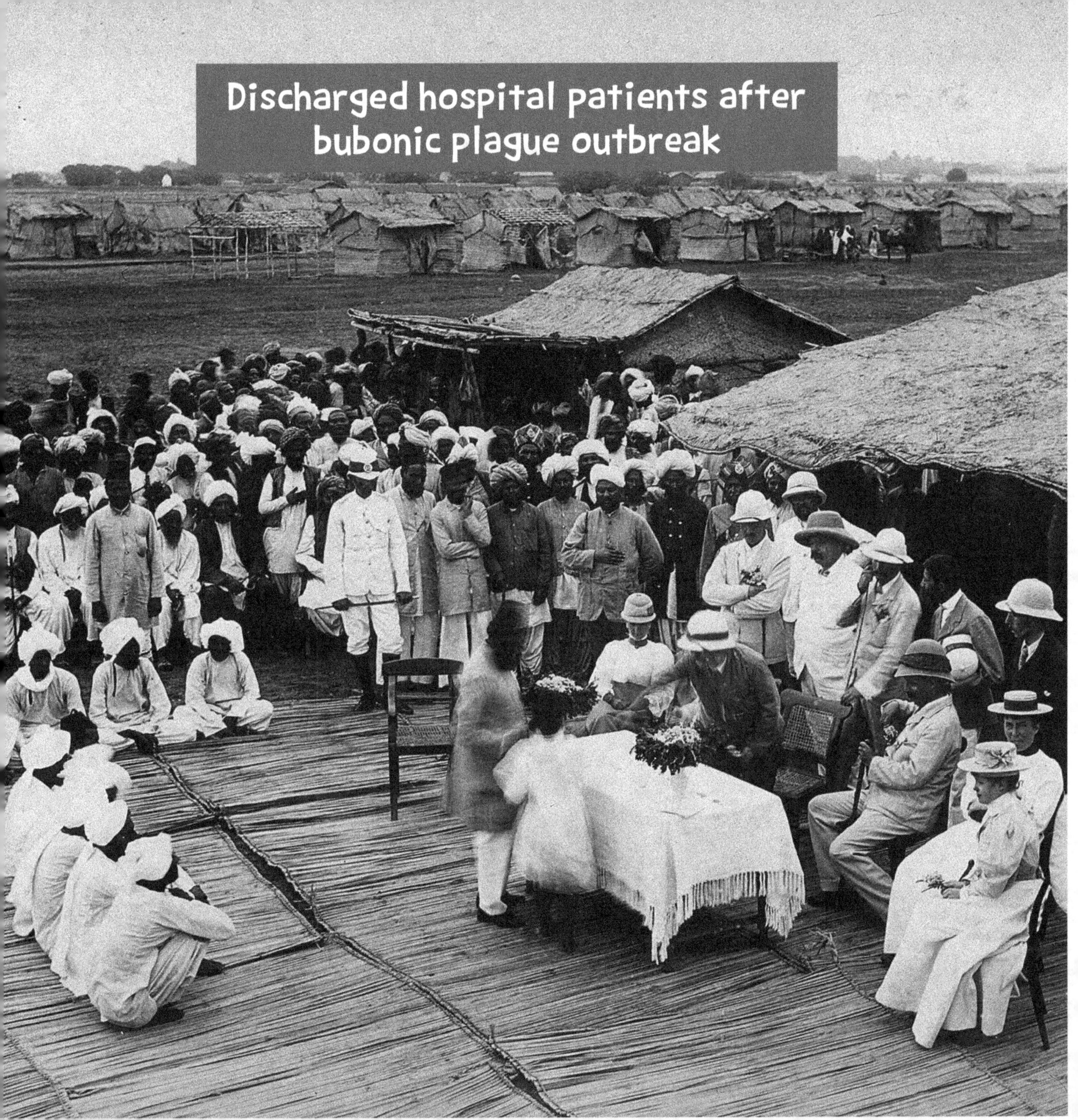
Discharged hospital patients after
bubonic plague outbreak

Middle Ages

HOW BAD WAS IT?

We can only imagine how scary a person's life was during this time period known as the Middle Ages. By the time it ran its course, this illness had killed at least a third of the European population, maybe more. It is estimated that approximately 800 people would die each day in Paris, France. They ran out of places to bury them since there were so many dead, so they carried them to enormous pits.

Unfortunately, during the Middle Ages, people had no idea that this disease had been carried by rats. Larger towns and cities, which were already dirty during this era, became even more dangerous because of the number of rats that were already there. Some entire villages and towns became wiped out due to the plague.

Trademan chasing a pig

Battle of White Mountain

WHAT DID THEY DO?

As one might have expected, panic ensued. Many felt that is would be the end of the world. They would lock their doors and try to hide inside their homes. However, this tactic didn't help since the city was full of rats, and their fleas were everywhere. Another attempt to stop this disease was to burn houses down, and in some cases, villages were burned to the ground.

Healthy people would do anything they could to avoid coming into contact with the sick. Doctors would refuse to see patients. Priests would refuse to even administer a person's last rites. Stores were closed.

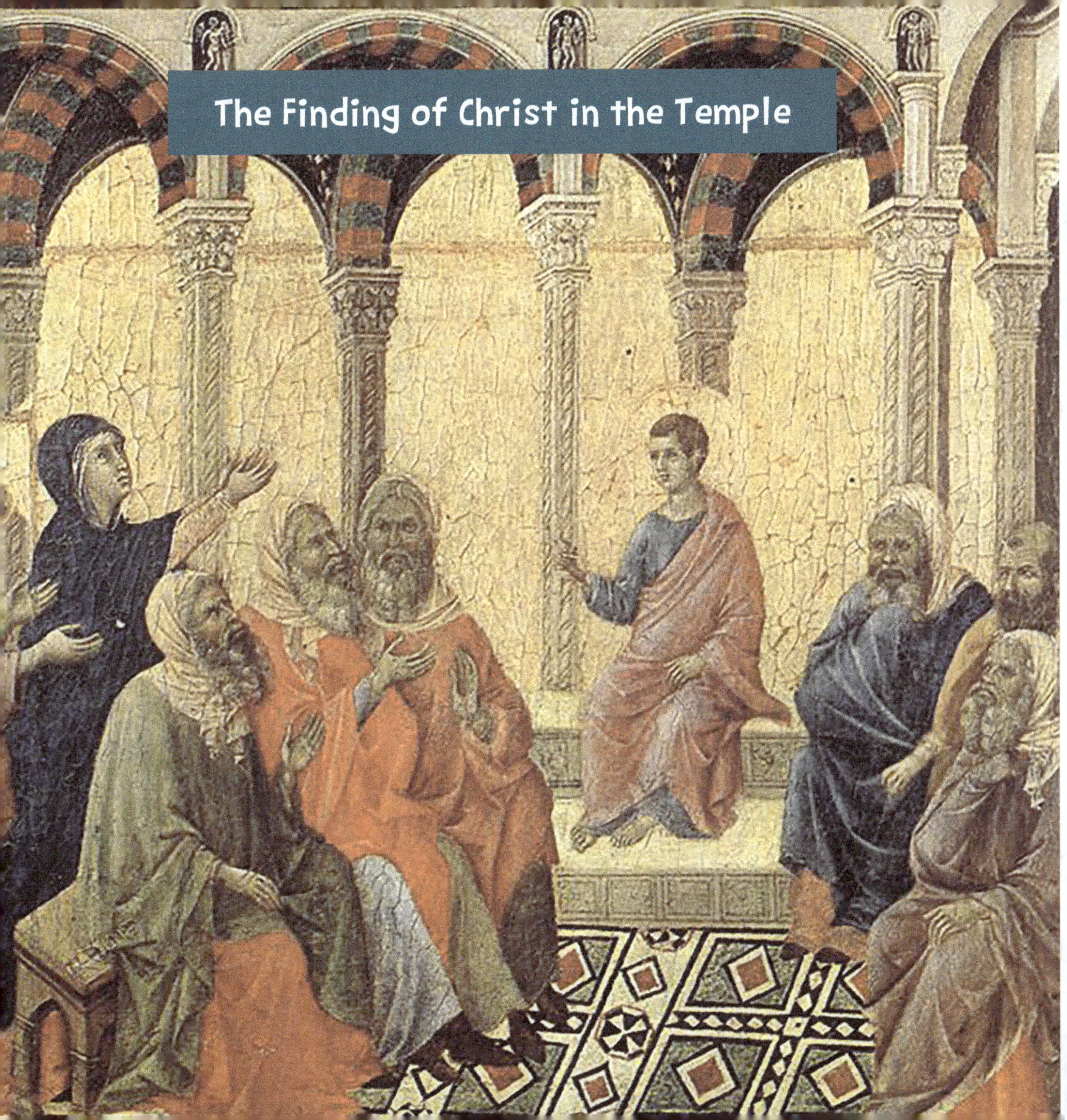

The Finding of Christ in the Temple

People during the Middle Ages

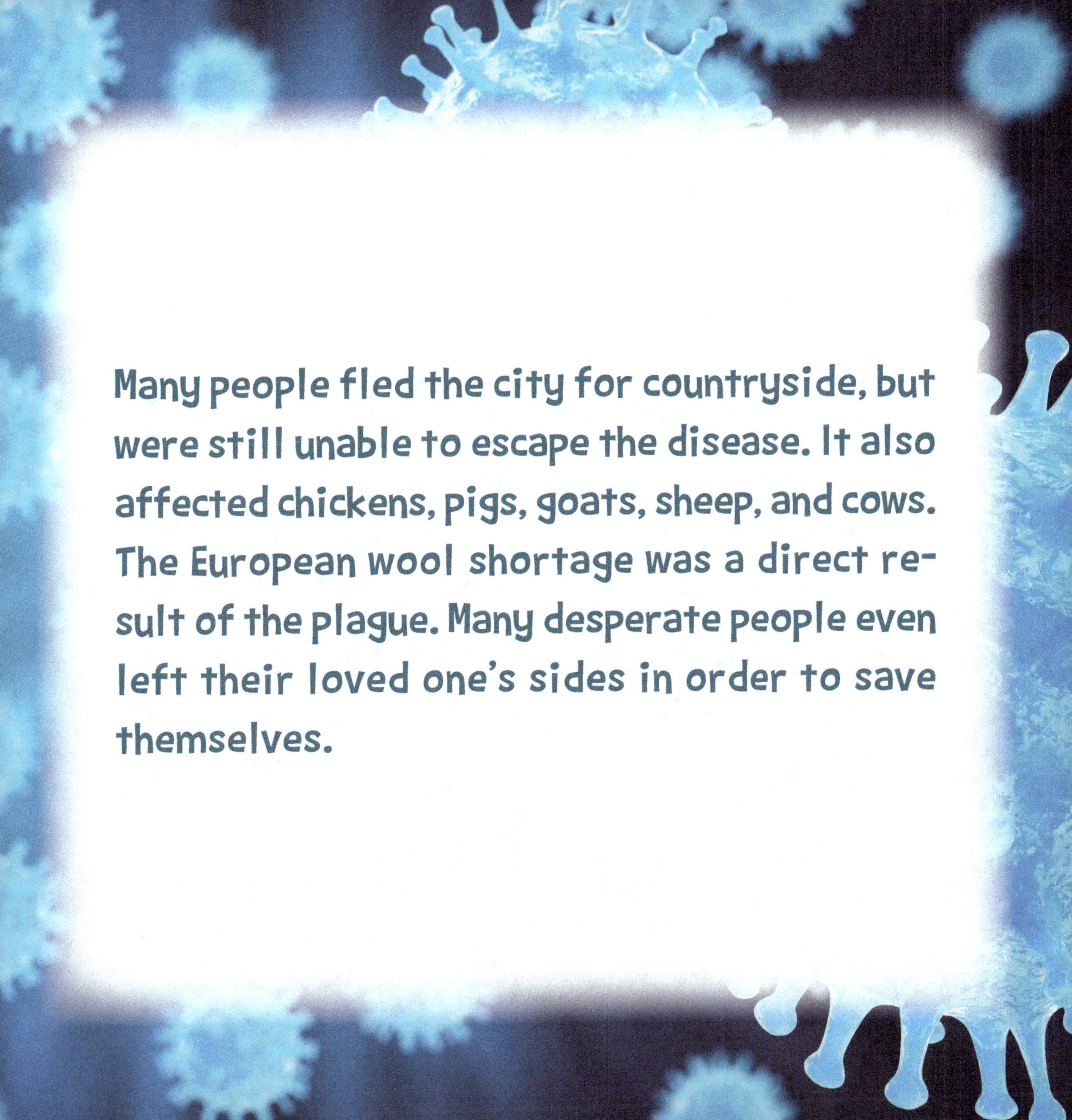

Many people fled the city for countryside, but were still unable to escape the disease. It also affected chickens, pigs, goats, sheep, and cows. The European wool shortage was a direct re-sult of the plague. Many desperate people even left their loved one's sides in order to save themselves.

WAS THIS GOD'S PUNISHMENT?

Since they did not understand this disease, many felt that it was a divine punishment – in retribution for the sins against God, including worldliness, fornication, heresy, blasphemy, and greed. Using this logic, only God's forgiveness would be able to overcome the plague.

Representation of a massacre of the Jews in 1349

Many believed that the only way to accomplish this was to purge the communities of the heretics and other similar troublemakers. For example, there were many Jews killed in 1348 and 1349.

Some dealt with this terror and uncertainty by lashing out to their neighbors; some turned inward and fretted about their own souls. Some of the upper-class men would join in processions that would travel from town to town, engaging in public displays of punishment and penance - they would beat each other as well as themselves with leather straps that were studded with pieces of sharp metal as others watched.

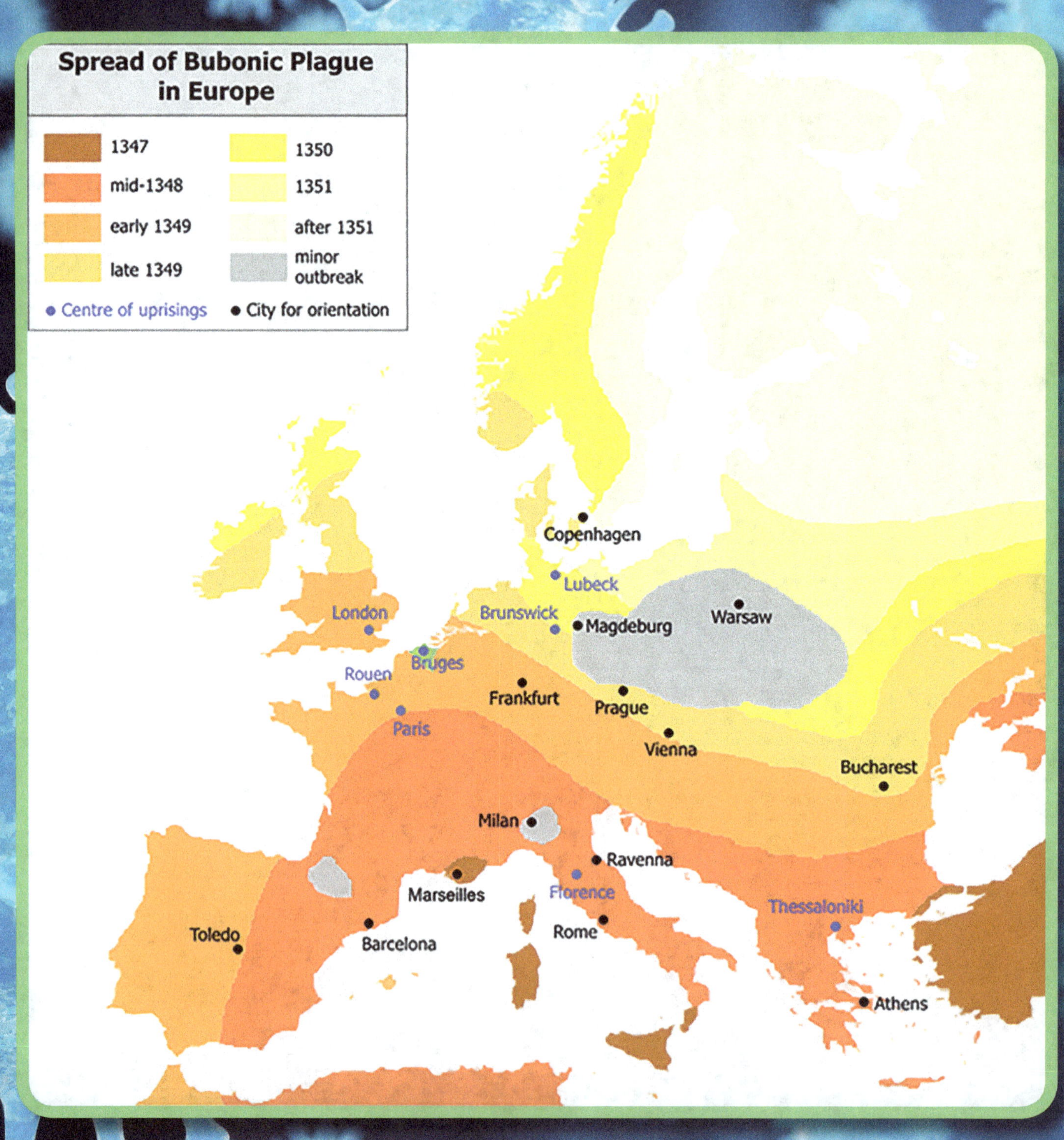

Spread of Bubonic Plague in Europe
1347
mid-1348
early 1349
late 1349
1350
1351
after 1351
minor outbreak
Centre of uprisings
City for orientation
Copenhagen
Lubeck
Brunswick
Magdeburg
Warsaw
London
Bruges
Rouen
Frankfurt
Prague
Paris
Vienna
Bucharest
Milan
Ravenna
Florence
Marseilles
Thessaloniki
Toledo
Rome
Barcelona
Athens

They repeated this ritual three times each day for 33 days. They would then go to the next town and start the process again. While this seemed to provide a bit of comfort to those who felt powerless, the Pope became worried. In face of the papal resistance to this ritual, it came to an end.

By the early 1350's, the epidemic had run its course, but would reappear for centuries. Public health practices and modern sanitation greatly mitigated its impact, but it had not been eliminated.

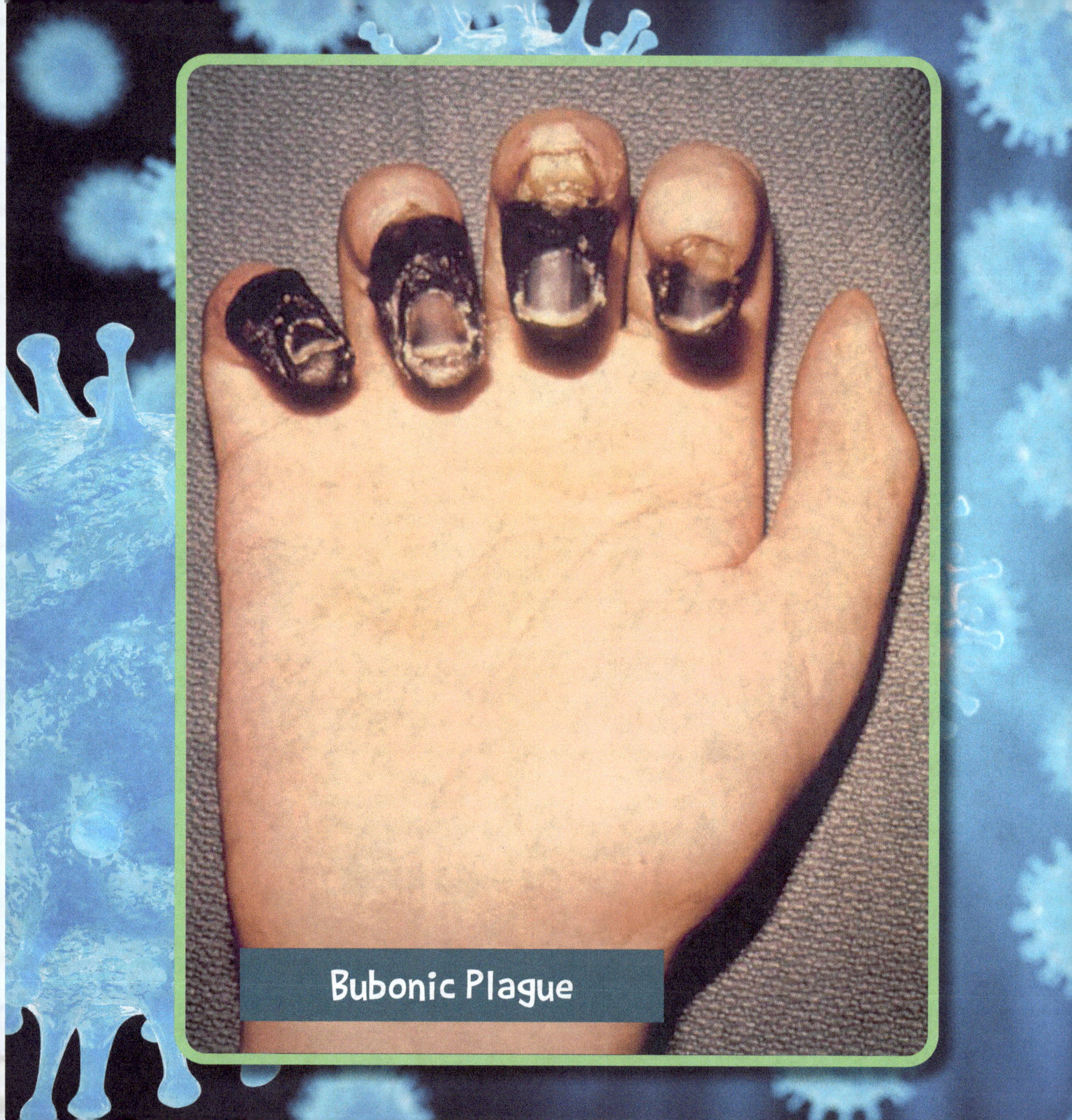
Bubonic Plague

THE BUBONIC PLAGUE

Today, the disease is referred to as the bubonic plague. It is rare that someone gets the plague now, and if someone does get it, most are able to recover very well. When someone got struck with the disease during the Middle Ages, there was not much possibility of recovery. They would become very ill with black and blue spots over their entire body.

It is a bacterial infection caused by Yersinia pestis. Once a person has been exposed to the bacteria, within three to seven days they will develop symptoms similar to having flu, including vomiting, headaches, and fever. The lymph nodes nearest to the site closest to exposure will become painful and swollen. On occasion, the affected lymph nodes may even break open.

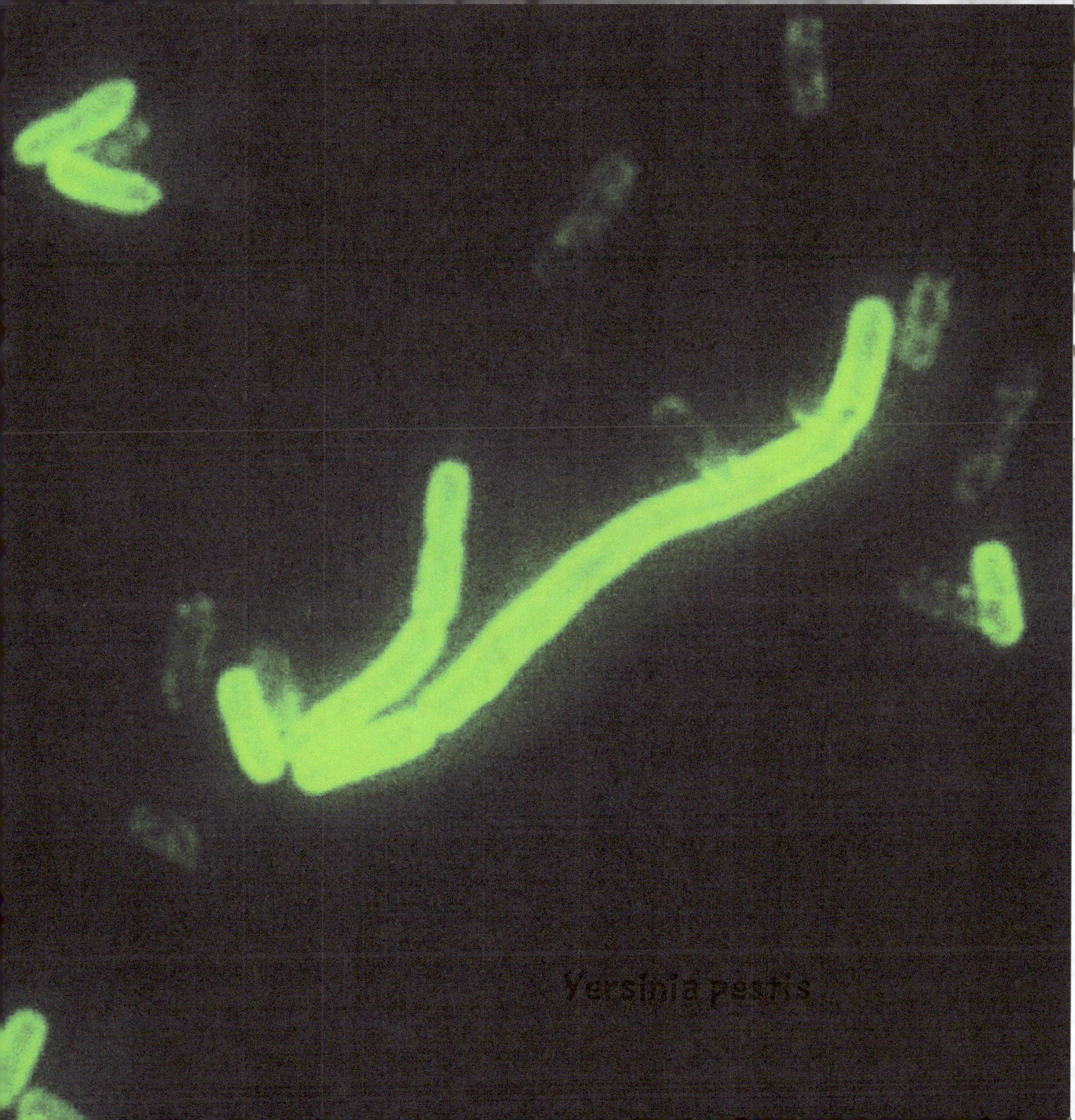

Yersinia pestis

Flea infected with yersinia pestis

The bubonic plague, pneumonic plague, and septicemic plague are the three different types of plague that result from the infection. The bubonic plague is typically spread by fleas and small animals that are already infected.

It is also possible to be infected by being exposed to the body fluids of a dead animal that is infected with the plague. The bacteria enter the skin through a bite from a flea and travels through the lymphatic vessels to the lymph nodes, causing them to swell. Diagnosis is made by the finding of bacteria in blood, sputum, or the fluid retrieved from the lymph nodes.

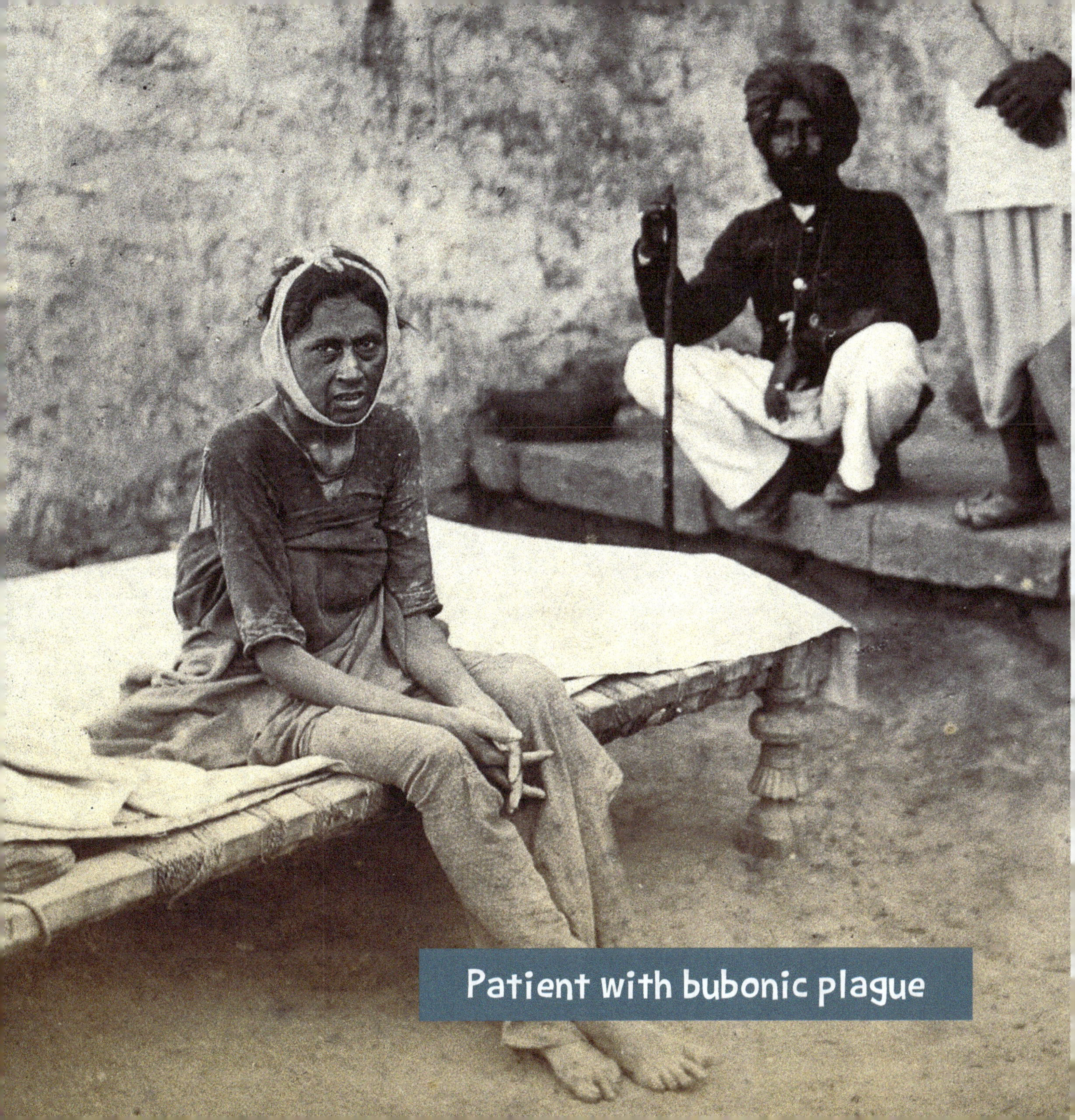
Patient with bubonic plague

Dead rats during the Bubonic Plague

PREVENTION

The first defense is to not handle any dead animals where the plague is considered to be common. Vaccines have been found to not be useful in prevention of this disease. Some antibiotics have been found to be effective include doxycycline, gentamicin, and streptomycin.

Death has been found to occur in 30% to 90% without any treatment. If death does occur, it will typically happen within ten days from the date of infection. If treated, the risk of death occurring is about 10%. In 2013, there were approximately 750 cases documented globally, resulting in 126 deaths.

Medical officer examining patients

Examining rats during the Bubonic plague

REBUILDING AFTER THE BLACK DEATH

Once the Black Death subsided, most of Europe's infrastructure had vanished. Reports state that it probably took around 150 years to rebuild Europe.

As discussed in this book, the Black Death was horrible and many people lost their lives because of it. However, with today's medical treatments, it is more than likely that you would survive if you became infected. For additional information, you can go to your local library, research the internet, and ask questions of your teachers, family, and friends.

Segregation camp during bubonic plague outbreak

Visit

BABY PROFESSOR
EDUCATION KIDS

www.BabyProfessorBooks.com
to download Free Baby Professor eBooks
and view our catalog of new and exciting
Children's Books